The Kids'
Library of
Personal Safety

A Kid's Guide
to Staying Safe on

BIKES

Maribeth Boelts

The Rosen Publishing Group's
PowerKids Press™
New York

Published in 1997 by The Rosen Publishing Group, Inc.
29 East 21st Street, New York, NY 10010

First Edition

Book Design: Erin McKenna

Photo Credits: p. 4 © Earl Kogler–Corp. Media/International Stock Photography; p. 7 © 1994 Kevin Anderson/MIDWESTOCK;  p. 8 © John Michael/International Stock Photography; p. 11 © Eric R. Berndt; p. 12 © B. Bachmann/Camerique/H. Armstrong Roberts, Inc.; p. 15 © Steven Ferry; p. 16 © Hub Wilson/H. Armstrong Roberts, Inc.; p. 19 © Robin Schwartz.
Photo Illustrations: p. 20 by Seth Dinnerman.

Boelts, Maribeth.
    A Kid's guide to staying safe on bikes / by Maribeth Boelts.
        p.    cm. — (The kids' library of personal safety)
    Includes index.
    Summary: Discusses the different types of bicycles available for children, how to select the best fit, and safety tips for riding a bike.
    ISBN 0-8239-5076-X (lib. bdg.)
    1. Cycling—Safety measures—Juvenile literature. 2. Bicycles—Safety measures—Juvenile literature. [1. Bicycles and bicycling—Safety measures. 2. Safety.] I. Title. II. Series.
GV1055.B64  1996
796.6′028′9—dc21
                                                                                96-48942
                                                                                CIP
                                                                                AC

Manufactured in the United States of America

# Contents

# Robbie

Robbie counted out his money on his bedroom floor. He finally had enough money to buy a new bike!

Robbie wondered if his parents would let him ride his new bike to school. Would it be too far? Were there too many busy streets to cross?

He tried on his brother's old **helmet** (HEL-met). It slipped around on his head. Was it supposed to fit this way?

It's very exciting when you get your first bike.

# Which Bike Is for You?

There are three kinds of bikes for kids. A one-speed bike is the simplest kind of bike. It has **coaster brakes** (KOH-ster BRAYKS), so it is easy to stop the bike. It is good for beginning riders.

A motocross bike has a small frame and special tires. Most motocross bikes have coaster brakes. This bike is used for racing or for riding around your neighborhood.

A mountain bike has hand brakes and wide tires. It also has different settings called speeds. You can choose one speed for going up hills, and another for riding on flat roads.

Many beginning riders choose one-speed bikes. ▶

# A Good Fit

To see if a bike is the right size for you, stand over the top bar of the bike. Keep both feet flat on the ground. The bike seat should be behind you. There should be a little bit of space between you and the bar.

To check if the seat is in the right spot, sit on the seat and try to **balance** (BAL-ents) the bike while keeping your feet on the ground. If you lean to one side or the other, the seat is too high. Ask your mom or dad to help you lower it.

◄ If your bike fits you, both of your feet will be flat on the ground.

# Should You Wear a Helmet?

Baseball, football, and hockey players all wear helmets to prevent head **injuries** (IN-jer-eez). Someone who rides a bike should wear a helmet too. A bike helmet protects your head in case you fall off your bike. Nobody expects to fall. But if you do, wearing a helmet can keep you from getting badly hurt.

Your helmet should not cover your eyes or ears. It should feel comfortable on your head, but it should not slide around or feel too tight. And you should always fasten the strap.

Try on your bicycle helmet to make sure it fits. ▶

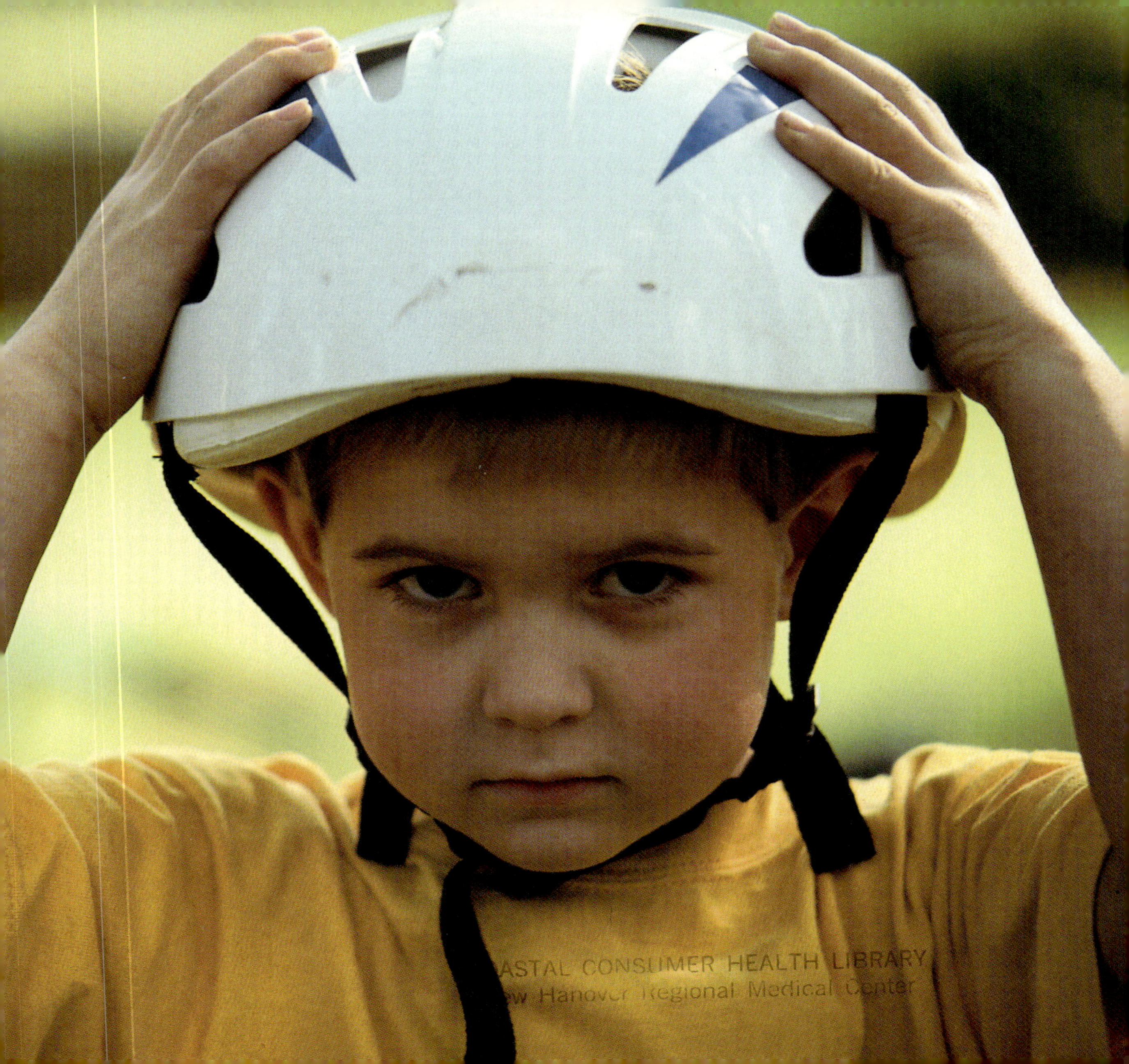

# Before You Ride a Bike

There are some important things to remember about bike riding.

- The law says that a bicycle is not a toy.
- Bikes are **vehicles** (VEE-uh-kuhlz), just like trucks and cars.
- You are a driver every time you ride your bike. You should follow the same laws as car drivers.

◀ When you ride, remember that your bike is a vehicle.

# Safe Places to Ride

Cars must drive on roads, where it's safe. Bikes need to ride in a safe place too. There are many safe and fun places to ride a bike. There might be a bike trail or park near your house. An empty lot can also be a good place to practice turning, riding, and using your brakes to stop at different speeds.

Even if you're riding in a safe place, watch out for other bikers, and don't ride after dark.

A park can be a fun and safe place to ride your bike. ▶

# Hand Signals

Cars use turn **signals** (SIG-nuhlz) to tell other cars that they are going to turn. You can do the same thing with your hands and arms when you are riding your bike. Use hand signals when you stop or when you're going to turn. This helps keep you safe by letting drivers and other bikers know what you are going to do next. Always use your left hand to make your hand signal before you make your next move.

◀ When riding with a group of people, hand signals will let others know what your next move will be.

17

# Crossing the Street

If you ever have to cross the street with your bicycle, stop and look in all directions for cars.

If you have to cross at a busy **intersection** (IN-ter-sek-shun), get off your bike. Take your time to look both ways before you cross. If there is a crosswalk, be sure to use it. When there are no cars coming, walk across the street with your bike on your right side.

Get off your bike when you have to cross any busy intersection. ▶

# If You Fall

If you fall off your bike, stay calm. Ask someone to get some help. A grown-up will need to see if you're okay. You may have a cut or a scrape that is bleeding. If you do, press on the cut with your hand to stop the bleeding. Sometimes when you fall you may get a bump or a bruise. An ice pack on the bump or bruise will make it feel better.

◀ If you fall, stay where you are until someone comes with help.

# Having Fun and Staying Safe

Bike riding is fun to do. You will want to keep your bike in good shape. Ask an adult to check your brakes, tires, handlebars, seat, and frame once a month. It's also important to carry and use a lock for your bike to keep it safe. You can **register** (REJ-iss-ter) your bike with the local police too. That way, if it gets **stolen** (STOH-len), the police will have a better chance of finding it.

Smart bike riding means knowing what to do and when to do it. Smart bike riding means having fun and staying safe!

# Glossary

**balance** (BAL-ents)  To be steady or keep equal weight on both sides.

**coaster brake** (KOH-ster BRAYK)  Brake used with bike pedals.

**helmet** (HEL-met)  A covering that protects the head.

**injury** (IN-jer-ee)  Harm or damage done to a person or thing.

**intersection** (IN-ter-sek-shun)  The place where streets cross each other.

**register** (REJ-iss-ter)  To write something on a list or record.

**signal** (SIG-nuhl)  Something that tells you when some action is going to start or end.

**stolen** (STOH-len)  Taken from someone without his or her okay.

**vehicle** (VEE-uh-kuhl)  Something that gets you from one place to another, such as a truck, car, or bike.

# Index